Mick Delap has turned to poetry after a working life with the BBC World Service in London. Born in 1942, his father was from Strabane, Tyrone, north-west Ireland, and his mother from the south of England. He grew up at her home in Hampshire, and was educated in Belfast (Campbell College) and Cambridge. First teaching, and then thirty years in radio, have taken him from his base in Greenwich, London, to Africa, south Asia and the Americas. His grandfather was born in Donegal but brought up on Valentia Island, Kerry, in south-west Ireland, where Mick shares a second home with his brothers and sister and his own children and grandchildren. As well as writing poetry, he is a member of the editorial group who founded, and now run the poetry magazine, *magma*.

RIVER TURNING TIDAL

RIVER TURNING TIDAL

MICK DELAP

Leanne
It was a joy to read
with you – best of luck –
and come back to Valentia!

LAGAN PRESS
BELFAST
2003

Mick
August 2004

Many of these poems first appeared in *magma*, to whom acknowledgement is due.

'My Father in His Nineties' also appeared in *Resurgence*. 'Search' was commended in the Blue Nose Poetry Poets-of-the-Year Competition 2000, and published in their winners' anthology, *Horizontal*. The following six poems won the prize for 'Best Collection by an Unpublished Poet' at the Listowel 2002 Writers Week, and were published in the Listowel 2002 Winners' anthology: 'Cromane', 'Kilrane Cross', 'Conversations With My Grandchild' (part 3), 'Deep Heaven', and 'Sea Cave'. The prize included a grant from The Ireland Funds towards the publication of this volume.

Published by
Lagan Press
138 University Avenue
Belfast BT7 1GZ

ARTS COUNCIL
of Northern Ireland

ISBN: 1 873687 99 0
Author: Delap, Mick
Title: River Turning Tidal
2003

Set in Sabon
Cover: Water/Stone (2000) by Maeve O'Connor
Design: December
Printed by Easyprint, Belfast

The poetry starts with people—Judy, the family, friends and welcoming strangers—and places. But these wouldn't have become the poems they are without the support of Laurie Smith, the *magma* editorial group and the fellow members of successive City Lit writing classes in London. In Kerry, Paddy Bushe has been a source of knowledge and inspiration.

... there will always be people,
... a ladder of angels, river turning tidal.
—Louis MacNeice, *Autumn Journal IV*

Contents

I

Heron	*15*
Cromane	*16*
Sea Cave	*17*
Deep Heaven	*19*
Reenellen	*21*
Famine	*22*
West	*25*
Kilrane Cross	*29*

II

River Turning Tidal	*33*
String of Pearls	*35*
Singles	*37*
Mobile	*38*
Aquarius Rising	*40*
Spring 1994, London	*41*
Bush House	*42*
Hunch	*44*
Translating	*46*
Search	*48*

III

Winter's Gift	*53*
Elements	*56*
Letter to Peter	*58*
For Sylvia	*60*
At your Funeral	*61*
December	*63*
Visiting	*64*
My Father in his Nineties	*67*
Greenwood	*68*
Conversations with my Grandchild	*69*
Agnes on Beginish	*73*
Voices	*75*
Leaving	*77*
Notes	79

I

Heron

Greenwich station. And
wearily off the evening train,
my eye is lifted to the hunch and push,
hunch and push of a heron overhead
shouldering aside the failing light
with laboured strokes that puddle
Dockland's gaudy, settling sky.

'Gooleyflap', my doting father
once hailed one with a sudden flourish.
Far from England and the ramshackle present,
back beside a childhood ditch in Donegal,
his flighty old man's mind
stilled itself, to strike,
transfix with a boy's wonder
the slippery, silver word.

And still, here in London,
this enduring heron draws tight
the burden of the day, lets go;
draws tight, lets go.

Cromane

I push through withered sedge, past upturned boats
wildfowlers have long abandoned to the rain,
and at the water's edge begin to scan
grey mud, grey lough, the marching sky's grey soak
for winter flocks of plover the murk still cloaks
in driving squalls. I hear them first, that run
of fluted calls. Then, before they can turn,
take off, they're there—and gone, like wisps of smoke.

I've lost them—and this incompleteness hurts.
Until far out over the empty lough
they wheel back into view. Like feathered sighs,
their fluent strokes relate swift air to earth,
wild sea to stone-walled fields, smooth to rough,
the trace of winter to a winter sky.

Cromane, Kerry, south-west Ireland

Sea Cave

Out where it first fists Europe,
Atlantic has hammered, salt-scooped
this sea crypt, cliff cellar,
from a fingered Irish headland. Today,
as I row in under a black wall of rock,
the cave's waters are lulled,
a bright lens on depths
of blue-white sea anemones,
red wrack, translucent parachutes
of jellyfish sinking faintly
through the membranes
of the deeper past.

My great-aunt rowed here, eighty years ago,
throughout the Great War,
to tow-net her indifferent specimens—
tiny medusas, budding hydra;
squeezing in like me, oars shipped,
past the pillared Altar Rock,
up to where the cave narrows
to the strange canals
smoothed deep under the headland,
pink-sponged, amniotic,
sucking salt breaths in
and out; in and out,
dissolving history.

Looking back, she would have seen
her green island framed for a moment
in rock, and flashing sea, and sun;
northwards, glimpsed Dingle across waters
that heaved Roger Casement
from his German submarine.
Easter 1916; and the night
the British hanged him as a traitor,

he wrote his mother
how he'd landed back in Ireland—
wading out of the sea
onto a dawn strand
fringed with primroses, violets.

Tremors in those quiet waters,
rumour of storm,
a distant quiver off the land
of tiny black seeds of poppy,
generations stirring themselves slowly,
redly, along the valleys: Laune,
Liffey, Lagan, Somme.

Where Europe ends, this sea cave
is still cathedral cool,
its hushed waters embracing
all we have committed to the deep,
and to the softness of corruption
and the mighty workings
of its salt-stained resurrections.
What lives on here swims
small and beautiful.
And as I back my boat out again,
past the Altar Rock,
warm sun strikes as a blessing
lazy sea, tiered cliffs, the immensities
of the oceanic West; and celebrates
each springing tide, each high,
each ebb.

Valentia Island, Kerry

Deep Heaven

i.m. Maude Delap, marine biologist, Valentia, Kerry, 1866-1953

Here in Valentia's fuschia-smothered graveyard
that gables the harbour mouth,
where ponderous Atlantic swells line up
and rise and detonate in turn, Maude's bones,
cabled in briar and hawsered by thick roots,
are surely ready now, picked over,
clean and white as one of her own fantastic finds:
the True's Beaked whale, the Porbeagle shark,
the Loggerhead turtles—all she buried
in the garden under the asparagus, then
resurrected, labelled, packed off years ago
as gleaming skeletons on the train
puffing slowly north-east, towards Dublin
and the waiting catalogues of the
Natural History Museum.

Ready—and here on the island
this day of glassy calm
could be the day she's waited for
to rise up and claim her own accession number—
this day where sea merges with the western sky,
gannets fly down into bright depths—
and keep on flying; pulsing jellyfish in sea caves
ring out their purple changes;
and her old parish church,
the hulk of generations, rocks gently
to the anchor that Hope, alert in the east window,
is ready at a word to slip.

Up the hill, in Jim O'Connor's hay barn,
her old black punt, its cracked ribs
patched and pitched for a hundred years or more,
stirs deep in its nest of brambles;
is reborn on a breaking wave of briars

that snags Jim, eighty-two and stiff
and grieving for the open sea,
sweeps him in a pother of gannets
and jellyfish and green leaves,
whale skulls, polished turtle shells and foam
up to the old graveyard—
where Maude's bones are young again
with a youth the young can only dream of.

And together they lift free, each seize an oar
and pull on the flood in perfect time north-west,
beyond the harbour bar, out past Reenadrolaun
towards the islands: Great Blasket, Inishvickillane;
small figures rising and falling evenly
on swells that break white against
the last rocky outliers: Foze and Little Foze;
on out of sight past Hy Brasil, the Blessed Isles,
towards that corner of a heaven
where the deep still teems.

Reenellen

Blown down last spring, a great cedar tree lies in the garden
that flourished, then faded with dying great-aunts.
Chaffinch and swallows are fooling today in the sun,
high in their perches on walls thrown awry by rain's
dribble, spray's lash, and the slow fall of years. Escallonia,
rampant, gives shelter to sun-seeking butterflies, bees
swagging a thicket of brambles, disorderly buddleia;
fragments of birdsong go skimming out over the sea;
boats swing in the tide. And swept up myself I sit
sprawled on the cedar my people once planted, walked under.
The gap where it stood is a desert of green; civility,
gentleness choked under briars, fallen slates, ruined lumber.
Yesterday, heartache. Today, fervent birdsong, bright sun,
flowing water. The cedar is gone, it's the sycamore's turn.

Reenellen House, Valentia Island, Kerry

Famine

This ancient church, set in fields
across a small creek, is where
great-grandfather must have preached
to the Famine's struggling survivors,
the victims of the wasteful ocean;
given each beached corpse the solace
of a slate headstone, dated
but nameless: KNOWN ONLY TO GOD.
And baptised my grandfather,
from the rectory the other side of the creek
that still looks back at mountains, out at sea.

In the churchyard, all the headstones
are skewed; the roof lies open to grey skies
and the neighbouring farmer's un-neighbourly,
spiky as the early gorse that glows
in his hedges and along the inlet
with its freight of kelp—which, now as then,
a Gallagher is harvesting. Seaweed, he says,
for want of anything more profitable
from sea or land.

By the time great-grandfather came here,
these Famine Walls between church and strand
were already built, great surf-smoothed boulders
piled grotesquely high to shelter hungry fields,
give starving families some relief
from the sea's old malice, the land's new spite.

Down the creek, the small breakwater
still stands against the endless rub of the sea.
It gave more work to those who stayed:
facing the quay with stone slabs, seating
the granite bollards; and setting the steps—
down which so many others left,

with farewells in Irish, or the rectory's English,
a last shared look over the stern
at quay and strand, airy mountain
and rushy glen, the little lanes
fluttering red, yellow, green.

Today the sky is granite hard and weeping sleet.
But the cliffs are softening again
in sheltered patches of primrose, bluebell,
and fresh knobs of golden gorse: *bláth an aitinn*;
its buttery yellow known to all
when butter was for most a distant dream.

Those Famine times are gone—
and many of us with them.
But we keep coming back, unsure
of what was left behind. We ask the seasons
how it was they turned, days
how they shifted. We wonder
how the seas still break, stones
still stand. And hear answers
in a speech we only dimly comprehend.

Out in the bay the outlying rocks still blow,
spout, seep foam in long curving lines
that once, my great-aunt remembered,
entangled a Spanish schooner. By sunset,
the seas had her ripped to matchwood.
And shattered homes desperate for timber, nails,
fastened thankfully on what the curling breakers
fetched ashore that night.

Next morning was quiet, bright.
But not as gaudy as the beach,
where waves so laden they could not break
rolled their bobbing cargo gently up the shore,
orange after round orange clustering in
until the whole strand glowed with them,

with something for which, till then,
there was no common word used in Irish
closer than *aiteann faoi bhláth*:
that yellow buttering of the gorse,
which glistens still above the strand,
as fresh, as constant as the rounded stones,
the shifting, unremembering sea.

Maghery, Donegal, north-west Ireland

West

I
Ray

The lodestone house,
far back, far West.
From the landward side,
the embrace of rough grey walls,
a vast fig tree greening the low door
which opened to the tarry tang
of a turf fire. Shabby, timeless comfort—
soft voices, soft oil lamps,
and glowing coals in the bare bedrooms
that sank into a stillness so intense
it sang all night with the bubbling waterfowl;
a dreaming not of absent noise
but present silence.

Day recovered turf embers
from the mound of fine ash in the Gun Room,
rekindled a trove of fragments washed in
by the wild Atlantic, and magpie generations:
pieces of sea urchins, tiny cowries,
curlew feathers, sea glass, a spinning wheel,
and a skein of family notices,
sheaved in letters, bundled up in gossip.

And day outside brought up the tide
across the mudflats, to plash
the shell beach, pinked with thrift;
splash over the bouldered sea wall
onto the house itself, its grey stones
dappled with salt and sun and lichen
and the purple shadows of the hills.

II

For Deirdre

When my Aunt Deirdre was eight,
Grandfather brought the boys in the family
steaming up to Belfast
from Ulster's green depths
to see *Titanic* launched.
Over more years, they flooded overseas;
only Deirdre stayed back
in Ray, far back, far West.

Grandfather and Grandmother were dead;
but from their walled garden
and beside the warm hearth,
my monkish aunt kept faith
with all of us. Grave, sandalled,
walking the shore with her cat,
hermit by choice, but sharing
the marvel of a tiny, folded shell, the unfolding
of a first seasonable flower. Inside,
deftly coaxing the turf fire to life,
sustained through low winters
by solid books, the wireless,
letters with strange stamps.

Summer again, she read us visitors 'Alice'
in a voice tuned to the slow harmonies
of the house, the three fields,
the passing tides. And the other side
of the disappearing glass, more secrets;
like her great-great-great-aunt's signature
diamond-scribed on one of the parlour windowpanes:
Anna (the Methodist), alongside a circuiting
John Wesley. And the crunch of departing hooves
down the gravelled drive.

The rising years washed Deirdre loose,
back to Belfast; old now, eyes sightless blue,
a stubborn mute sucking toothless
on the salt tides she invited
to flood the years and flood the miles
between the slowly turning present
and the empty house
far back, far West.

III
Compass

My last visit, I searched in vain
amongst the rubbish in the wrecked parlour
for fragments of the signed window glass.
No *Anna* as the purple light
died on the hills and another tide
edged back over the mudflats,
chasing the curlew, forcing the heron
awkwardly into the air.

There was kelp untidy along the shore—
when I first came to see Deirdre, aged four or five,
some were still gathering it
in high-wheeled carts, for the fields,
or to burn for cakes of iodine;
as others had in great-grandfather's days,
when the potato was failing
and the coffin ships waited on the lough
for the lamenting families.

Now Deirdre, stranded like them
on distant memories, is cold
as Ray's ruined hearth.
All failed, all gone
from homes that wait on

like empty, roofless tombs.
But journeys are from
as well as to; and these
are compassed places, compassed lives.
Their being warms our own beginnings,
points us still.

Kilrane Cross

While the band sets up,
lorries straight off the English ferry
rumble by on the new road like dreadnoughts
under the sodium lights—
or pull in here out of the sleet
with the Mercs and the mobiles
for scampi and chips—and the first tune
   Is long mé, méas aim:
      a ship I am under cargo, under sail,
         with no haven before me

two grave old men flying along on accordions,
upright and deliberate in ties and sweaters,
one bald, one white-haired,
while a scrawny, apologetic fellow of a drummer
thumbs the bodhran, and the only one
still with the dark hair he was born with
taps away on the spoons
   a book I am written in the sky,
      no one to understand me

A few claps above the chatter—'Florida or Boston?'
World Cup, the latest Tribunal dirt: 'Would you
believe the neck of the man?' And a halt
while drinks are set.

Then one of the accordions eases into
   My Love Is In America,
a fine thread of a tune that's picked up,
given weight and shape by the other,
   urgent legs by the bodhran
   A stór mo chroí: beloved of my heart

The bald, thick-necked accordionist
sips delicately at bright pink lemonade,
they all share a joke, fly off once more
  The Humours of Whiskey,
    Mother and Child

and the bald one's intent, eyes tight shut,
head bent over the squeezebox in his lap
that's taking him out the back door
  The Chattering Magpie,
    Carolan's Farewell

into small lanes deep in winter gorse
where the Mercs never venture.
And a late blackbird's lonesome touch
sings him towards Mulrankin,
Tomhaggard, Kilmore Quay,
the room where he first picked out
  Head O'Cabbage,
    May Morning Dew

and the smoky kitchens he set alight with
  The Bucks of Oranmore,
    Phil the Fluter's Ball,
      I Buried My Wife and Danced on Top of Her

They end with a flourish
and he opens his faded blue eyes
on distance and strangers,
not one of them dancing.

Kilrane Cross, Rosslare, Wexford

II

River Turning Tidal

Cycling with the traffic
from Waterloo towards the Strand,
I stop at a red light
where a man and his young son
hesitate, so the anxious father
can consult his London tourist map.

Like me, they've just crossed a bridge
that does not any more connect us
with its ends or its beginnings,
a river that somehow does.

Behind us on one bank,
the spoils of distant war,
echoes of cannon and cavalry,
British Grenadiers in squares;
somewhere just ahead,
a long-lost beach, phantom tides,
the splash of Saxon oars;
but louder than either,
the *ooohs* and *aaahs* mid-river
from the grandstanding crowds
when we first packed today's more concrete span
to launch the Festival South Bank—
fireworks overhead reflecting colour
back into our upturned, post-war faces,
smoking salvoes re-echoing the Blitz,
cannoning forward off the coming Silver Jubilee,
Millennium; backwards again
to earlier Jubilees, VE, VJ,
Mafeking—and Waterloo.

The boy at the traffic light
is only five or maybe six;
hears none of this; raises

his face earnestly towards his father,
sure that map and parent
have all the answers.

When I was five,
my father brought me up to London,
ran for a moving bus beyond my reach
and hopped aboard.
I watched him pull away—
and howled him back to me again.

The trick worked then. Today,
looking at father and son beside the lights,
I know the map turns blank,
the bus will pull away, and the boy
must face the traffic on his own:
routes, crossings, shortcuts,
hurt spaces

where the river, mapped mid-flow,
engages with the hard corners of the city;
lays down a begging arm,
bent, palm uppermost, slack.
Only for each sharp bridge
to slash it pink,
each pointed spire to nail it down,
haemorrhage the spreading stain
down tide;

while the boy that was,
raising his head one day at dusk,
will find himself back on this city bridge—
upstream beyond the Wheel
a lingering sun; downstream, he knows,
the darkening sea.

String of Pearls

I

Fahrenheit 451

The year's begun in heavy frost. Just one
South Bank bookstall's stayed open long enough
to see dusk squeeze day early out the door.
I pick up a Jungian *Guide to Symbols*, read
of Prometheus, how the gift of fire
'allowed a hairless, furless animal
to settle in a hostile wilderness'.
Balding, in woolly mitts, the bookseller's hunched
against the cold and the dark river's rising,
a stubborn beacon of enlightenment.
But the book's so bad, I dream of looking back
under the bridge to see him chuck it
on a pyre of duds he warms his fingers at.

II

Vermeer's Milkmaid at the Tate

Paint
brush
canvas.
Pouring maid—
pouring milk, herself
into the serene light that pours
itself over bread, basket, wall, and goes on pouring.

III

Thinking Haikai

Meeting for haiku—
high in the Festival Hall
syllables falling.

We were shut in a side room
across from the closed main hall.

Shut this mid-week autumn night,
it listened vast and brooding.

As you did by me. Present,
but absent. Found and still lost.

While through the plate glass windows,
glimpses of the ebbing Thames.

A string of light bulbs—
restless water reciting
something dangerous.

Singles

Love-fifteen. So far, still sharp in my mind—
autumn sun, bright shadows, how sweetly
you moved that last shot past me, by how much
I missed! *Love-thirty*. Now I'm serving again, wishing
you'd miss me more often. And you do, this time—
fifteen-thirty (so odd this courtly language). But
sod me! that one smoked past. And I grunt fiercely,
claw back to *deuce*, *advantage*, *deuce* again.

Off court, three magpies, a flight of parakeets;
my right foot aches inside new trainers; leaves drop.
But I forget what aches of yours—or how you won
those points I lost? Even the score—still *deuce*,
égalité? If only! The other side of the net's
a pilgrimage away. It started, I recall, *love-all*.

Mobile

Departing KING'S CROSS
he was the dark-haired man
with the folding bike, half hidden
in a corner seat. Then
as we moved up a gear—
Arsenal's stands soaring into the murk
beyond the trackside waste—
he produced his phone.

Before we got to FINSBURY PARK
grey steel, gleaming new glass
elbowing flat-brick terraces
we knew he was Douglas,
easing out of KNEBWORTH
the train bursting through fog's dreary hoop
out into sun-spoked fields, our windows
snagging radiant hips, bright haws
Douglas Robertson: thirties, close-cropped hair,
light pleasant voice, and clearly
doesn't mind the carriage knowing ...
WELWYN at speed
that he lives in Epsom,
leaving POTTERS BAR
silver flash of willow, moorhen
caught out, scrambling for a ditch
has a two-year-old—and ...
slowing for BALDOCK
sharp autumn sun illuminating
oak's tawny parchment
prefers to cycle. Next year, though, he hopes to fly,
on the 21st of May, to New Orleans—alone,
for business. But then he'll meet
the rest of the family two days later,
in San Francisco. On holiday.
If the fare's right—and includes the air miles,
all twenty thousand of them.
And that's a must, he says.

By ASHWELL & MORDEN
a concrete chimney pluming its steam downwind
across the coming green of next year's corn
grey seasoning of pigeons
Douglas reckons we're more or less on time
for his morning meeting, ten o'clock,
in Cambridge; tells someone else
he's sure the moment isn't yet right
for clinical trials. But later in the week ...
somewhere between MELDRETH and SHEPRETH
willows and ditches and sky, more sky, more time
than the radio astronomers' poled array
can hope to riddle, sieve
... later, he'll be seeing
Doctors Northcliffe and Stott
to discuss Gonzalo Martins Gonzales,
who he's referred for further tests.

By FOXTON
we even know his number,
095 double 7, 1 double 3, 456.
Plus, he dials left-handed.

But as we all spill out at CAMBRIDGE
into a milky field of autumn light,
the lawns glittering, worn stone
warming, and those green shoots
behind us now, the two-year-old,
the tiny seeds pith deep
within the shining hips and haws
Douglas, struggling with oil-stained fingers
to unfold his bike, suddenly appears less sure
about what really happens next.
Or where. With phone switched off,
tucks trousers into clips, straightens
in silence, like us, to face the town.

If I were Gonzalo Martins,
I think I'd keep him on my case.

Aquarius Rising
for Miriam

Now you're eleven, and I'm fifty-three.
On your Cambridge doorstep,
mine for a while, Newton
built his Mathematical Bridge.
Without nail or fastening
shaped timbers arc across the measured Cam,
a fitting proof
of gravity.

The dark frame, the slatted planks
rise up and out
to where we lean and lightly contemplate
our element below,
its slowly turning willow leaves,
its milky flow.

This bridge is strong on theory, firm in fact.
Like these black letters laid across the page,
it orders what it joins.
But through the slats between our feet,
and from the space between dark words,
whiteness wells up,
diamond sharp and dangerous,
infinite in its endings
and its beginnings.

Where it gleams,
tugs and throbs in the blood,
you will follow.
All I can tell you is:
days darken into night,
answers come hard,
but the journeying shines.
Please, let me know.

Spring 1994, London

South Africa's first ever multiracial elections

Outside my Greenwich door,
winter's regime of black and white
each week concedes more ground,
until one splintering night
the cherries up and down the street
hoist their pink flags; a blackbird
signs the bright articles of dawn,
coins a new day.

Just two weeks on, the cherries are in tatters,
their petals fallen; at first reluctant,
then showering down to lie in drifts along the kerb—
puddles enamelled pink, drains clogged;
this spring tarnished as soon as any other,
but different in the one affirming act:

that millions, black and white,
the patient, burdened old, impatient young,
have joined together far from here,
stooped down toward the drifted blossom,
and having each picked out their own fresh-fallen petal,
have delicately smoothed it in their palm,
so they can mark it with a cross
and place it reverently
between the pages of the moment.

Bush House
BBC World Service radio, London

By day, the official cycles
of despatch, assertion, and denial
chase each other noisily in
for the bulletin's public judgement—
weighed in the newsroom, hurried
from screen to studio; red light:
headlines that bark back out
above tense chatter in the cubicle,
restless waves of traffic
washing down the Strand.

But when day here ebbs, quietens
with these emptying streets,
then faint messages spark
through the dark, pilgrim stories
searching the world for sanctuary.

Small cries of love, the weep of hunger:
how in the Gulag this man survived
by watching beady-eyed
where tunnelling rats cached
their winter rations.

Messages of loss, of what can be endured:
the black woman in South Africa, nervous
with her new voice, insisting all the same
her humbled masters return to her
at least a finger of her abducted son.
One finger—so she could one day hope
to close both their lives in the same grave.

Stories of wonder: how long carpets
billowed like sails across mud floors
in the earthquake, as a laden donkey

flew up into the air and showered in its wake
a great tail of dried crocus petals.

And murmurs from the voyagers,
from the frail harbours of the derelict,
calling, recalling home.
Small whispers from those
who have resisted silence,
always believing they would one day
celebrate their lives again with others.

And here, in the quiet of each Bush night,
their witness is taken up, and amplified,
fused into a banner of sparks
that soars up into a darkness
turning back to noisy day, as a red bus
trundles the new dawn in from Greenwich.

Hunch

This morning's shower looped crystal drops
along the phone lines sagging
down my Greenwich street.
April, which celebrates green openings,
stays shut for me. Across my desk
just a scatter of holiday snaps
that blaze *Namib*, 'desert':

where last night a pack of hunting stars
dragged down the sun to let sea fog
roll in again across the dunes,
blanket the gravel plains behind;
moon lands bleeding shards of agate,
brittle with orange lichens
desperate for a suck of the drifting mist.

Below, dry water courses nurse
the distant memory of flow;
a camel thorn sweats out a drop of dew
for the rough tongue of an antelope;
and soothed from the fog, a smear of liquid
seeps down a slab of marble
towards the pebbles at its foot—

which stir with dawn, unclench,
reveal themselves as *lithops*, living stones,
colour, sap and seed pouched up
against a hammer of a sun
that's already sent the stars packing,
ripped mist to shreds,
and now is bricking up what's left
in the furnace of its day—

out from whose blazing heart
a swivel-eyed chameleon
blinks, stalks forth at noon,
a Shradrach-like survivor;
past an untidy pile of leaves
crouching unconsumed in the wilderness
like one of Nebuchadnezzar's queens.

Wild-fingered, -haired, a *welwitschia* plant
older itself than Babylon
splays from its prehistoric womb
two endless leaves, dull green,
time's entrails, whose extremities
frizzle to unpicked raffia
as they hit the fiery sand;
over three, four desert-millennia
have stretched out from this one plant,
unravelled; stretched out, made way.

Back here in Greenwich, blackbirds' casual song
adorns each parapet, water flows carelessly
towards spring's easy leaving.
But I stay brittle, dry mouthed.
While the *welwitschia* pursues
its three thousand year old hunch:
gritty, thrawn, awaits the next subtle shiver
far below; then, like a straining, ancient windlass,
inches new life from some deep-buried core;
clacking it up, pawl by pawl,
through aeons of gravel, sand's dead blanket,
towards the searing light. Ekes out
more green.

London / Namibia

Translating

for Princess Sayyida Salme, 1844-1924

I am a stranger to this northern summer,
its waves of aqueous green, alien shoals
of birdsong, ambiguous scents.

Tonight there is a sea turtle
gasping in the bath.
Outside, the stamp, jingle
of a waiting cab horse;
guttural shouts from a drunk sailor
off one of the steepling clipper ships
furled hull to hull in dock.
Beside me in the bed,
my husband mutters strangely.
What does a man dream
who has married a Zanzibar princess
and sailed her home to Hamburg?

And what does our domed turtle dream?
Plucked mid-ocean from her star-mapped sea,
penned on a slanting deck, while each night
ever more alien constellations
unrolled before her beaked gaze.
Until one day the deck settled, stilled,
and she was knocked down, dockside,
to be tomorrow's first fruits,
at our first ***da'awat asha'a***,
which I must learn to call *Festessen*, 'dinner party'.

Tonight my turtle fins feebly, dreams with me
of the same hot sands, harsh light,
the vanilla-scented crack of bursting pods,
fragrance of cloves far out to sea
beaconing beachward.

Tomorrow I must close her nostrils
with my stark 'yes': *Mach' das*; 'do it!'
On our warm island, wreathed in spice and subterfuge,
there was no need for language
when my husband came to me;
no veil between us when I breathed 'yes'
to his urgent body, 'yes' to his love.
And he is a good and simple man. My *Mann*.
But beyond his caring arms, the coldness
of his distant friends, his catechising God.
And all I bring, my shivering, unveiled 'yes'.

Soon that will be 'yes' to ***al-maut***; *Tod*;
my daughter-turtle's death.
Freeing her homing breath to wheel
with the stars across sweet waters
to remembered sand.
While I stay grounded here
in the dry channels of my mind.
And dusty by me on a mantelshelf:
a domed shell, emptied
of all but lamentation.

Search

freeserve.com RIGHT CLICK
and the air thickens a little,
spins tighter SEARCH *floods*
SEARCH *Africa* CLICK *February two thousand*
TEXT *Limpopo* SLASH *Mozambique* ENTER
sheets of water ... miles of water
wash thousands from their homes ...
worldwide concern
CLICK *pix* CLICK
tree

Tree? Tree,
a four-days' ark
above the greasy waters
spread across everything familiar
with the swagging clouds, the drench.
Sanctuary for two by two: two kids,
two parents (the mother pregnant,
swelling with the flood).
Over the expanse black birds,
but bearing nothing in their beaks,
soon gone; shouts, cries early on,
and once, day two, over the monotone
of falling rain and swirl,
the distant thump of a helicopter,
unseen, fading to silence.
Day three, the gripe of hunger,
the tree shivering at night
with the tug of circling debris,
the black flood's stillborn bumping past.
And dawn, day four lurching
with the mother's breaking waters,
cresting pains, cries, shaking
knuckle gripped, and suddenly

the child dropping
in a thunder of arriving wings,
the torrent of downdraft whipping
the water to spindrift, whipping the tree,
and the pluck, the clean pluck
of rescue, up spinning
through the branches into air,
the tree suddenly diminished,
islanded, gone.

CLICK *tree* CLICK *world*
there was a second helicopter
a cameraman SEARCH *flood mother*
CLICK *Sophia Pedro, twenty-six*
SEARCH *baby* CLICK *Rositha*
SLASH *family: husband Mundine (no age)*
Benet, three, and Celia, five.

From all our TV screens
Rositha bawls, smiles off front pages
in her mother's arms. Their hut
(in an unnamed settlement
near somewhere at the world's beyond
called Mondiane) is gone,
and somewhere out there in the bloated flood
their ten chickens, ten pigs.
But Sophia and Rositha are happy,
and so are we.

So CLICK *exit* CLICK *shut down*

Never to know more
of their river's quieter noises,
how the dark waters reflect for them
the brighter stars, strain
to capture the fainter gleam
of a winking satellite;
never to know even

what kind of tree it was
that rooted their baby's life.
Casuarina? Fever tree?
Or *mpondo ndlovhu*?
which the Europeans call 'lead-wood',
but which translates better as
'the tree as old as the elephants'.

And fade to black.

Limpopo River, Mozambique

III

Winter's Gift

This winter moves me like a gift
late in coming.
Its terror is beautiful,
like the beginning of terrible deeds.
—Osip Mandelshtam, December 1936

Covent Garden well after dusk
still stuffed with Christmas shoppers
driven by the contradictions of their lists.
Beside the towering, tinselled tree
three Chinese buskers, improbable
in square spectacles and suits,
splash yearning notes up off the black cobbles
into a moonlit lake of sky.
And as the ripples die away,
the dark-needled tree itself begins to sing;
deep in the branches, light-throated starlings
declare themselves like chiming candles.

Years ago, the candles
set our Christmas tree ablaze.
Father, home from the war,
threw my brother's new tweed jacket
round the flames, hurled
the smoking bundle like a slung comet
out through the window.

The brittle cold of other Christmas nights
was lit by stars like great magnolia
snagged high in the silent elms—
against whose rough bark
you first announced the hot smoothness
of your lips. Of lips.

And there was still the softer flame
of treble voices singing of a child,
and all the perpetual possibilities

of a child. The holy days of Christmas,
straining like Mary
towards an understanding.

For half the world, the shortest days.
Far out beyond all suburbs
at the untidy margins of frozen fields,
old angels with tawdry wings
have heaped up the ambiguous present.
Bare winter trunks whisper in charcoal
down a grey page *(even the ravens*
are alarmed by the leafless circle);
freezing fog has bandaged light;
and the mid-morning sun looms up
like an immense headlamp.
Hoarfrost has beaded the season's litter
in crystal. It glitters briefly, crunches under foot,
and is submerged as light moves off,
and dark *(like a gift late in coming)*
flows in behind.

This Christmas is my father's eighty-fourth.
In the house in the village
the bejewelled husks of last summer's tortoiseshells
are scattered on his window sills;
by day, the low winter sun
taps weakly on his dusty window panes,
by night, he drifts alone down dark waters
(the bulging blue of half-formed ice),
past misty fields, dim thorns,
a tentative thrush singing
of hard and bitter agony,
a bloody birth and a thin cry.

Soon, the boomerang sun will circle back
to knap this dull earth to brilliant shards,
sharp-edge another year of dawns.
There will be easts rimmed eggshell blue,

a gold line seeping pink, upswelling
harsher, more gold, and bursting through
to dazzle cold ground with leaves—
a promise for the hurt of thorns.
There will be a child's believing fingers
round the driven nails; and thrush
to answer thrush.

For now, dark hedgerows wait
to crucify the dying light.
Only the holly, bottle-green, blood-pricked,
ignites the spent season, the last colour
drained with the drifted leaves.
No light to warm soft flesh,
to candle youth; no saving wing.
Only the necessary wound of dark.

And as the cold earth slows,
it is a moment for a child,
and for the hardy cattle
kneeling at midnight in the fields
like humble kings. Absence
rises like an unsuspected mist;
the missing haunt all loss;
ice dusts the silence of the end of years.
And only my enduring angel,
only a seeing heart
can tell how small it is,
and how immense—
this gift of winter.

Elements

i.m. Betty Delap, 1912-1983

Water

At dusk the river's flow
takes on a black solidity
like liquid jet; a whispering pendant
unclasped at evening's end and folded
in the silver-stoppered crystal jar
that in the day still splashes
sunlight like a stream
across your dressing table.

Air

Ten years ago you died, Mother,
here in this still room above the water meadows.
That frozen night, knowing already
it was too late, we chased the snow
in flurries over the Downs.
The house was warm downstairs;
above, you waited your release.
And when I climbed the stairs
and touched your waxen face,
it was alright.
On the blown curtains of the blizzard,
you had become once more yourself.

Fire

In those last awful weeks,
your spirit smouldered like the angry core
of some clinkered star.
In ghastly parody, turned midwife
I pressed your swollen stomach
to help you pee. Good speech
was what you always valued most,
but even that was taken:
through the slag in your throat,
push, you rasped, *push*,

while your blazing heart,
which had seared you
as much as all of us, illuminated
for one last hungry look
all it had so brilliantly ignited.
Above us in the attic, layered in a case
like delicate flakes of wood ash,
old letters from a lover
I never knew you had.

Earth
After your funeral—a cremation
with little left to burn—
we all went sledging on the Downs,
grown children and grandchildren
hurtling down in a spray of snow and ice.
The trees threw back our shouts;
and tumbled at the bottom
we brushed off tiny crystals,
fire frozen in perfection,
and looked back up through
stripped beeches to where
the native yew trees stood, rooted
in dense thickets whose ancient darkness
outshone the fading light.

Water
Dimly sensed, on the other side of the water
small birds settle for the night
among the willows.
There have been hills, the wider sea;
for now there is this chalk stream
glinting in the dusk,
its slow surface stippled
by falling rain.

Letter to Peter

At tea, spent, you said
you couldn't cope with another visit now;
held tight the doorpost as you waved goodbye.
So here is how, next day, I spent
your gifted morning, walking alone
(my legs, your eyes) under high hills
wrapped in swift cloud,
Borrowdale singed with autumn
and the glint of ribboned streams.

From High Barrow Bridge, the long haul
up Breasthigh 'Road', a sodden unkempt track,
and down into Bretherdale with the run of waters
sluicing green summer off the hills; sheep soaked,
the gates down into Bretherdale Head
reeling awry, tied up with baler twine,
a rusting trailer chassis in one corner of a field.
And in the deserted yard, a musty caravan,
door swinging; out back, a young collie
tethered to an oil drum kennel,
barking wildly at the stranger.

Hard farming, neither looking for favours
nor expecting them. On the retreat.
But these are the folk you doctored for years,
won over by turning out all weathers,
starting with those treks through breast-high drifts
in nineteen forty-seven.

This day under a wilderness of sky
the Beck's running dark and loud
past Head Farm, down from
the tangled hillside thickets
where a few red deer still harbour—

their wildness hour after hour
your solitary healing study.

So when, cutting back up from the dale
through thick forestry, I'm suddenly
face to face with a stag, two hinds,
I sense your presence too. The deer
melt back under the canopy of spruce,
but the stag halts, half turns, head high,
to size us up, dark nostrils questing.
A snort, and then I'm looking at
a steaming cloud of breath,
hanging, blown.

Nothing more—just the long haul
home over the thin-grassed tops,
flensed small by a high, cold wind.

And that's my autumn day—your day.
As winter comes, you're leaving us
on our own to face the hills
at the end of obscure, steep-sided dales.

Up the old tracks, if we can find them
in the low light, a single hawthorn
grips the edge of the high commons
by the beginnings of a stream that
falls back down towards us
through an ancient wall.

And somewhere up beyond, a stag,
mud-caked, dun-coated,
enduring stubbornly.

For Sylvia

celebrating her 80th birthday in St. Petersburg, Russia

Pushkin loved autumn—those first Baltic gales
roaring through the oaks, sandpapering
their leaves to parchment, sharpening
the edge of loss. And the colours, fading slowly—
like those snaps, eighty years' worth,
in your drawingroom back home
beside your own great oaks: the sepia country vicarages,
Box Brownie tea parties on Dorset lawns;
flashbacks in black and white to a slim Wren
surrounded by young men from submarines
that slipped from sight beneath wartime waters,
were gone. But always, and in technicolour,
those shots of the one who did come back,
and kept on coming, building with you
a noisy life enlarged by daughters,
classy yachts, improbable dogs, wild schemes.

Now, you've had to choose the latest dog
yourself, hold the first great-grandchild
on your own; but still, as the young step out
into your garden's light, you follow lightly,
tidying away another autumn's leaf-fall,
planting for another spring.

At your Funeral

i.m. Dorothy Grenfell Williams, 1935-1994
BBC World Service producer, and Head of African Service

At your funeral, Dorothy, summer's swirling wind
invented improbable destinations for the leaves,
dizzied the squat steeple against fleet clouds,
tried to dissuade us from the sheltering porch.

Inside, doors shut, the quiet order of tall pews
and all the formal furnishings of loss
struggled with grief straining to join
what ravened through the graveyard,
heaved at the doors, breathed hoarsely
against the windows.

Outside once more, only inbound jets
rumbling overhead, only sparrows teasing the laurels.
And a dazzling wind that tugged us
toward the open grave.

Huddled by the wreaths, we gulped
the sobbing air, watched mesmerised
your coffin stagger past, hesitate, lurch,
fall in. The gravedigger threw off his coat,
leapt after, to grapple in the clay with coffin straps.
But still, on end, head first, it slithered
down the breach of time, detonated

absence. In that moment your loss
towered up in silence from the cratered grave.
Grew, terrible, to blast the laurels, rend the yew;
reached high to rupture
the deafened membrane of the sky,
topple gravestones, shred leaf and petal,

sweep up our slivered memories
and pierce us with each keen fragment;
still in slow motion, scythed
through the rippling crowd, knifed deep
to mangle summer, scatter us bleeding
among the trampled flowers.

The coffin rescued, summer and wind flowed back
to scatter spent wisps of grief and give us breath.
We straightened, and resumed;
laid you to your even rest,
clattered fists of soil, fluttering petals
on the still coffin, and moved away,
clutching at wounds like medals
whose spreading stain would stay
and bloom again, again.

December

This time of year subdues the light.
Walking on the sea marsh,
neither midday's muted sun
nor the estuary's spring tides
will ever shift this holed barge again.

Beyond its grounded bulk,
a flock of peewit takes to the air
in patterned flight; with every buoyant stroke
winking from black to white;
a pause, and back,
back from white to black, winking out
over grey mud flats towards
the silver cord of the sea.

Far behind, the barge's sodden timbers—
and the only gift on offer this Christmastime,
a glossy flight feather, shed.
No sudden buffeting of fantastic wings,
no lifting miracle of tides;
only this feather, cast off,
abraded at its tip.

Visiting
for Miles Delap

To be with you again,
a son for the weekend,
I pedal over the Downs into the village,
catch my breath before your door,
and brace myself. At eighty-six, the lines
linking you to this season,
mooring you to all the others,
have gone slack, slack as your face
adrift behind the oxygen mask
last year, while your waterlogged lungs
threatened every minute to swamp you,
and your wild eyes signalled panic.

I never saw you whip a rugby ball
from the scrum, nick the bails
from behind some batsman's indignant back,
lift Mother lightly off her feet. But later,
along the rocky shoreline of a mountain lough,
I watched your wrist fuse mind, arm and rod.
The line curved away in the heather-scented breeze,
connecting you surely with the water's glittering surface,
the peaty depths, the little trout
rising silver to the fly.

Well into your seventies,
those wrists commanded the same elegance
from the red dinghy you rowed round Beginish,
Valentia's 'small island', or the penny whistle
you milked at night for jigs and marches,
just as they had mastered the racketing machines
you flew with such amateur delight
through the uncomplicated pre-war air.

War's cannon shells
speared your Blenheim over France.
They killed the rear gunner,
turned the burning cockpit
into a spinning, roaring womb.
As the red stain spread,
the navigator found you stunned,
midwifed you out through the hatch
into the buffeting airstream,
somehow pulled your cord before his own,
and left you floating for a silken moment,
suspended like one of your own trout flies
between one element and another.

Before you slid back feet first
into the luminous green resonance
of a May wood. You never told me,
can't remember now, whether the ground fighting
had silenced the birdsong. But as you crawled out
you noticed that fabulous summer
had left the bordering ditch bone dry.
You also picked the right side
to exit from, and to—
next year I was born.

Now I'm on your doorstep,
wet, but more afraid of your foolishness:
whether you'll be wearing five pairs of pants again
against the chill, or none;
what story you'll get stuck on,
tell, re-tell, five times an hour,
while the gaps glaze over
the deep pond of your mind
with the first fragments of what must soon
freeze me out forever.

When I was five, you shinned up a tree
to rob a magpie's nest,
conjured fire and an old tin can,
and hey presto, scrambled eggs!
Today, our roles reversed, I wonder
if it ever seemed to you as simple
as you made it seem to me.
I think it did. There was a beauty in your skills
which you accepted without question.
Just as you now accept their loss.

From outside, the house is dark.
You've gone to earth,
a tired old fox, burrowing deep
against this cold in the bone.
When I dig you out,
you'll sport a jaunty grin,
but we both know
how few tricks there are left.

Behind me, as I shut the door,
rain droplets glitter on the whitethorn:
crystal beads, unstrung,
each one a random lens,
distorting, clarifying, dropping.

My Father in his Nineties

My father in his nineties,
a keen-eyed country boy
who flew up from an Ulster parsonage
into Europe's blazing air—
and landed in this wheelchair;
all his long life leading
to this unravelling. He's
lost his bearings,
touched down God knows where,
but still knows how to look about—
hungrily at the ground
for an odd-shaped pebble,
sweet paper, dandelion;
then towards the horizon
for a benchmark tree;
then up, up, to the birded,
liberating sky.
Oh yes, then, quizzically,
at me.

Greenwood

Spring's tightly wound. Song spirals out
from woods re-learning early green;
a buzzard circles over trunks
still winter bound. But primrose, hyacinth,
an early butterfly, intoxicate
with colour, scent, new warmth
on skin long winter scanted. Growth
rings through clearings still bare enough
to see back in beneath the trees,
beyond what's fallen by the way,
to where beginnings root themselves.
Before uncreasing leaves, a surge
of bluebells swell this tracery
of folded buds into high summer's
walls of green. And spring runs down.

Conversations with my Grandchild

I
Christmas Eve

Christmas Eve, day waning
towards midnight's singing door—
while deep in these sodden woods
lunatic Canada geese still honk
on a muddy lake margined by shouldering trees
seized now by a damp gust,
now by leaf-moulded silence—

through which the smallest birds
flit like daystars in the high tops,
ardent in their patterned intricacies
of tiny beak and feather and intent.
Spring-loaded, winter-locked,
a nuthatch chisels, treecreepers
hang off alpine crevices of bark,
a minute goldcrest dainties
like a jewelled pocket watch.

While you, three months in my daughter's womb,
are only as big as they, according to the scan
I've stuck with the other cards
on the mantelpiece. And there you nestle,
curled up like winter
in these stricken woods.

II
Midsummer

Six months on, the woods are heavy
with midsummer's various outcomes.
Today's green wave has buried
winter's broken things, launched
all but you, still skulking
great in your mother's womb.

Last night I waited under a near-full moon,
glowworms policing the dim edges
of the sandy track, white moths
blundering the sweet-smelling dark—
before they fell to the gape, the sudden snatch
of nightjars hawking the leaf-fresh air.

By this far sheltered wood you dawdle,
formed, but not yet ready for this impatient world,
where knowledge storms from leaf to leaf,
and ancient differences take laser-guided wing.
When it is time, I want the trees
to leaf for you—be more than refuge,
more than an image on a screen.
And in good time, may you bring
your own child to them.

III

for Agnes Schade Delap
at her christening, Nikolai Kirche, eastern Berlin, 7th November 1999

We are laying hands on you today,
parents and grandparents,
signing you in our different tongues
with the waters of our faith.

You're small in our hands—
but your own are still smaller.
When you were born, in those first hours
when you were still dreaming your way
through some elemental sea,
not yet come properly to land,
you would open your milky eyes
and gaze around for a moment,
like a seal pup popping up its dark head
before slipping back down, out of reach.

Even so early you could hold, hang on.
Mostly though your intricate, tiny fingers
stayed limp, unstrung, somehow still unconvinced
by the snatches of music, laughter
drifting towards you off the shore.

For the first two days of your life
your Delap great-grandfather, ninety-four,
hung on with weakening grip,
falling back towards the same deep waters
with shallow breaths like yours
that hardly troubled air, the same limp hands.
Unreliably present. But here with you,
until he quietened, slipped under, went.

Your coming is a green wave
washing the hurt spaces where he walked.
You've shifted Berlin next door to London,
made a gate for each of our two families
into the same garden.
But in those two overlapping days
you also linked an old man's years
with all that lies ahead of you.

When he was young back in Ireland,
young as the old century, his soft hands
curled around his German nanny's finger,
sieved Atlantic strands for cowry shells,
the amber-flecked water of a bog stream
for silver trout—while your East Prussian ancestors
beachcombed for proper amber
cast honey bright on Baltic sands.

Twice in his life, our countries turned
to fight each other. For more long years
a wall kept us apart. Until that night,
ten years ago, when the people

pushed it down. And west and Clare
met east and Peter here.

Now we are in Berlin again, together.
And you have come, Agnes, spinning towards us
like a stone sent skimming, skipping
over water. You dip to kiss silver,
rise faster, dip again—and rise to air
off all these waters,
all these streams.

Agnes on Beginish

It's a short haul from Valentia
to the low, small island, Beginish,
but the sea is troublesome today
and our dinghy pitches, slaps

as you sit solemn-eyed, cauled
against your father's chest, dazzled
by the glitter off the water, waves
that break themselves, re-form, re-shape.

Halfway across, I saw him
dip a finger over the side
and plant a baptismal drop of salt
plumb on your forehead,

touched now with the homing salmon's
hot leap to wisdom, the steady pull
of islanders, McCroachans, O'Connells,
the Caseys most lately—and earlier Delaps.

We land on an empty island.
Jim Casey's in his grave, and Mike is waging
whiskey wars with his niece on the mainland.
This May, Beginish must announce itself to you,

shake out its yellow flags, late primroses,
pink thrift; show off white sheep and whiter lambs
against lichened walls, a lark-grazed sky,
the breaking shiver of the open sea,

which whets island lives to an ever thinner blade,
a whitened bone half buried in the sand,
the carcass of a lamb bleached, still fluffy, on the turf,
a gannet broken-necked and rubbished by the tide

that's down, and leaves us slicked beach
to race across; you screeching in my arms
for joy, too small, too young for the cold stab,
maul of the upending surf,

which once we've gone will quickly wipe
our prints. But may some scent of yours,
some sea-charged trace remain behind, to call
and keep on calling to your salmon mind.

Valentia Island, Kerry

Voices

A romance of the sea, the pilchard fishers, and the twins Esther and Lucas Schade Delap (read at their christening in St. Nicholas', Deptford, London)

Sea was first. Sings softly to itself
far out beyond the weather off the land.
And still the shoals' soft answering,
dreams dreamed together

as the little fishes spin
with sun and tide and clouds, until
like a purple shadow, a stain
on the waves, they come.

These are the sea's old voices.
Here on our rocky land
we fishers murmur as we wait
for the shoals to come to hand,

till 'Heyva' we cry, 'Heyva',
as the waters stir. And we
seize the long seine nets,
set thole pins for our oars,

pull out to scoop the silver fish
in thousands, tens and twos,
into our salty vats, into
the barrelled press.

I am now Lucas
I am now Esther

Before, we dreamt in millions, millionths,
all one with wind, sea, shoals
and sun. Unthinking
and unthought.

Until your nets' embrace
brought us to you,
and in your barrel's press
we slowly somersaulted, formed;

like Doubting Thomas, Thomas the Twin,
learnt from each other's touch
the growing wound of life
swimming into, out of our dreams,

the dreams we have dreamed
still dream
as two,
as one.

And out you flopped,
the two of you, in time!
Each neat as one of our little pilchards,
with arms you slowly waved
like a sea anemone's fronds,
vague dreaming faces,
drifting eyes. Still
all at sea.

Now you have launched us
back in the stream,
the font of St. Nicholas,
Thames at full tide.
But fast in the cords
of your faith and your love.

And far offshore
where the unnamed still dream,
the small breaths are moving
the waters, the light.

Leaving

At boarding school in Belfast
they fleered my Englishness,
back in Hampshire
guyed any hint of Ulster.

But the school's great avenue of beeches
unfolded every May a fragile green
that matched perfectly what I'd seen earlier at home,
the jasmine's delicate response to winter.

Notes

West (p. 25): Deirdre Delap, 1903-1999. Ray house, Lough Swilly, Donegal acquired by James Delap in 1716.

String of Pearls (p. 35)
(i) Title used in London to describe significant attractions along both banks of the Thames.
(ii) *Vermeer's Milkmaid*:Word count of lines increases in accordance with the Fibonacci mathematical sequence, as do many examples of natural and artistic beauty and harmony.
(iii) *Thinking Haikai*: In seventeeth-century Japan, an individual haiku could be linked to other haikai by a series of fourteen-syllable couplets.

Hunch (p. 44): *Living Stones* are succulent plants of the genus *Lithops*. They resemble small stones, until the desert conditions they live in relent enough for them to put out their solitary yellow or white flowers and succulent leaves. *Welwitschia* are a mysterious plant unique to the coastal deserts of south-west Africa. Discovered by Frederic Welwitsch in 1860, the precise mechanisms by which they survive desert conditions remain unsure. They put out just two large, continually renewed leaves from a woody stem; a single plant may survive for over a thousand years.

Translating (p. 46): Princess Sayyida Salme was born on Zanzibar Island in 1844. The ruling family, of which she was a member, spoke both Arabic and Swahili. She married a German merchant, moved to Hamburg, and wrote the first book to be published in Swahili. When she died in exile in 1924, she was buried in Hamburg beside her husband.

Letter to Peter (p. 58): Peter Delap, 1913-2002.

Visiting (p. 64) and *My Father in his Nineties* (p. 67): Miles Delap, b. Strabane, Tyrone, Northern Ireland, 1905; Royal Air Force 1928-47; d. Hampshire, 1999.

For Agnes Schade Delap (p. 70): The tenth anniversary of the fall of the Berlin Wall was 9th November, 1999.

Voices (p. 75): Pilchards are a north Atlantic sardine. Their shoals used to be caught in enormous numbers off Cornwall. A few still are.